UNLEASH YOUR Greatness

A Guide to Transforming Your Life
Through Your Authentic Purpose

RACHEL HALE

BALBOA. PRESS

A DIVISION OF HAY HOUSE

Balboa Press books may be ordered through booksellers or by contacting:

Balboa Press
A Division of Hay House
1663 Liberty Drive
Bloomington, IN 47403
www.balboapress.com
1 (877) 407-4847

Because of the dynamic nature of the Internet, any web addresses or
links contained in this book may have changed since publication and
may no longer be valid. The views expressed in this work are solely those
of the author and do not necessarily reflect the views of the publisher,
and the publisher hereby disclaims any responsibility for them.

The author of this book does not dispense medical advice or prescribe the use
of any technique as a form of treatment for physical, emotional, or medical
problems without the advice of a physician, either directly or indirectly. The
intent of the author is only to offer information of a general nature to help
you in your quest for emotional and spiritual well-being. In the event you use
any of the information in this book for yourself, which is your constitutional
right, the author and the publisher assume no responsibility for your actions.

Any people depicted in stock imagery provided by Thinkstock are models,
and such images are being used for illustrative purposes only.
Certain stock imagery © Thinkstock.

Here is how you can get in touch with Rachel Hale:
Website: www.therachelhale.com
Email: info@therachelhale.com

Print information available on the last page.

ISBN: 978-1-5043-6886-5 (sc)
ISBN: 978-1-5043-6888-9 (hc)
ISBN: 978-1-5043-6887-2 (e)

Library of Congress Control Number: 2016918223

Balboa Press rev. date: 11/21/2016

Contents

Dedication

To the best Mum & Dad in the world x

A Note from the Author

I write like I speak.

That means this book maybe a little bit different to what you're used to.

You won't find any grandiose, flowing paragraphs, and I'm breaking the rules that my English teacher said I should never break.

Self-expression has always been a massive part of me.

That means if I write I have to feel free.

If I speak I have to feel free.

If I eat a darned chocolate cupcake I have to feel free.

Why on earth would I want to try and fit into a grammatically correct and utterly dull way of expression, when my heart and soul yearns for the kind of freedom that breaks all bounds that I know you also feel?

This book is made up of 2 parts.

The first part is about my not so perfect journey into discovering greatness, losing sight of greatness and rediscovering greatness.

The second part is about how you can discover your own innate greatness, give yourself the permission to unleash everything that you know you are born to be.

Life becomes so much simpler, easier, happier, and far more fulfilling when you ruthlessly cut out the distractions and focus solely on what matters.

Your greatness matters.

Beyond anything else.

Some people will pick up this book not even sure what this whole greatness thing is about.

It's not a word we use everyday in reference to ourselves.

But I know that the word, Greatness, resonates with you somehow.

At a deep level.

That's why you're reading this book.

I will not waste your time, I have far too much respect for you and for myself.

I want to be able to show you why you feel such a connection to this word.

I want to be able to take you on a journey to show what's possible, no matter where you are.

This book is about stepping out of the shadows, and finally recognising the version of yourself you've been hiding under wraps.

The version of you that bedazzles.

The version of you that changes lives daily.

The version of you that heals the brokenhearted with the power of your message.

The version of you that is happy and fulfilled to its very core.

You'll find out why you've been hiding.

Things will start to make sense.

You'll find that once you know what's possible that your appetite for this adventure will be insatiable.

Then I would have done, what I came here to do.

To show you why unleashing your greatness is what you came here to do.

With Love

Rachel x

PART 1

Chapter 1

Revenge of the Underachiever

"You'll never amount to anything".

The teacher announced from one end of the classroom. The silence that followed seemed deafening to my ears.

I was standing up, amidst a sea of heads, and about 50 pairs of eyes burning holes through my skin.

My hand was still stinging from the corporal punishment meted out to me by the classroom ruler, that dreaded dispenser of justice, a minute or so ago.

I hadn't done my homework to the teacher's satisfaction.

I think I was supposed to cut out pictures of vegetables and paste it on a cardboard, but as far as I can remember I didn't have enough vegetables to show.

I was 8 years old.

It makes me deviously happy now, to think how my teacher got it all wrong.

But at the time, she certainly made it clear that I was an unpromising child, not bound for great things in life.

After my initial public humiliation, I decided that I WAS going to amount to SOMETHING.

Partly because I wanted it, partly because I wanted to prove her wrong and mostly because I was far more ambitious than my teacher could have ever imagined despite my shortcomings.

See...I've always felt it on the inside.

Not in a cocky, or arrogant sort of way, but in a way that helped me look beyond the multitude of random people, dotted throughout my life, who had the audacity to tell me how my life should be, what I should say and how I should act.

I've felt greatness.

I've felt that I was born for greatness.

It was a feeling that came from deep within that felt as if I could trust my life with it.

I knew.

I somehow also knew from a young age, though I can't say I fully understood it back then, that greatness needed expression, and without expression, it would wither, it would retreat to a dark corner of your soul, and it would not see the light of day for years to come.

Greatness needs nurture to come into being, and doing what makes your heart sing and feel alive with freedom has a lot to do with the "How To" part of unleashing greatness.

As far as I can look back into my childhood, I remember being able to sing from about when I was 3.5 years old.

If I heard something on the radio, I did a pretty good job of memorising it and singing it, or rather humming it, on pitch and with gusto, according to my Mum.

I don't ever remember LOVING singing. I have to borrow a quote from To Kill A Mockingbird, here to explain.

"One does not love breathing".

It was so natural, I didn't think about it, it flowed right through me like breathing.

It didn't take effort, it felt like it was the most natural thing I could do.

I didn't realise how much I loved it until later on when I hit a dreaded writer's block and entered into a soul famine that sucked the creativity and happiness from my life.

Anyway getting back to the story at hand, I grew up to be a quiet, yet observant and a curious child, who did more singing, dancing, acting and any other form of expression which felt completely natural to me.

It wasn't a part of me. It was ME.

It took me a while to figure out but it was my way of expressing the greatness within.

To sing, to dance, to act, without a care in the world.

Unashamed and unbound self-expression.

Without any need to re-think, manipulate, follow a strategy, build a business or a career plan around.

I've always felt that everyone has greatness within them but unless you grew up in a home where you were 100% nurtured and allowed to be who you are, we all eventually learn to forget and let go of our greatness as we grow old.

It's like we come into this world as perfection itself and slowly through nature and nurture, teach ourselves to move away from our own inherent greatness.

Ironically we also get caught up in a lifetime habit of perfectionism trying to FIX the part that we feel is broken so we can get back to being whole.

All of a sudden, acknowledging your greatness in any shape or form, becomes a faux pas, and the adults admonish us with "Don't show off, be polite, let others have a go, don't say it like that, you're not special" and so the list continues.

So you start off with perfect confidence, and before you're a toddler most of that is whittled away from you.

This process continues and creates such a confusing vortex of disconnection within that the angst that it creates by the time we hit our confusing teenage years can be life-altering to say the least.

Some of us barely made it out alive from that period.

See, as a child, Greatness used to feel natural to me. And then I made the mistake of growing up.

Basically I decided that I was no longer that great.

Why?

Well...all sorts of reasons really.

People told me I wasn't that great. Refer to my teacher episode at the start. (and it only increased from there)

I found out that what I did was never quite good enough. (Cue, confidence being eroded away by an onslaught of other people's opinions)

I was just alright, nothing that impressed the average observer, in fact it took a few greatly perceptive people to realise the gifts, the compassion, the sensitivity and love I carried within.

I was easy to doubt and dismiss.

Standing at 5 ft 4 it's difficult to be impressive.

I was out of touch with what I have always known to be true, and felt as if I was now no longer good enough.

It drove me to adopt a habit of perfectionism, that would destroy my creativity and happiness many times over before I learned the lesson.

There was a lot going on at the time...

Society told me that I was just another face in a sea of faces, and I can't stand out unless my skin colour was a fair bit lighter, and quite frankly unless I looked a little bit more like a girl.

(See...I was a quintessential Tomboy, a skinny little stick figure and a mite of a child. People sometimes mistook me for a boy.)

I was that girl who loved playing with dolls, but did it while wearing jeans and a baggy Guns n' Roses t-shirt.

Yet even as my world was changing, I was blessed with some moments that would leave a deep mark on me, and give me an unshakeable sense of self, and an ability to know that I was here for a purpose and that my own greatness lay hidden within me, ready to unleash.

I remember one particular incident from when I was probably around 10 years old.

My Mum was a Teacher at my school, respected and loved by her students for her incomparable intelligence, wit, charm, beauty and grace. She was strict too.

So here we were standing around with a few other teachers, my mum and I, and inevitably the conversation turned towards me.

One of the teachers remarked that my Mum ought to make me dress up in a more feminine manner, I suppose to disguise the fact that I looked like a little boy, and that I ought to act more like a girl or I will be stuck in this predicament (being a tomboy) for the rest of my life.

(She probably had visions of me being a 100 year old tomboy spinster, wearing my Guns n Roses t-shirt and jeans)

I stole an anxious look at my Mum, feeling disappointed and angry at myself for being a cause of embarrassment for someone like her, who was revered, utterly beautiful in all her feminine glory and fierce as a lioness to boot.

She never so much as looked at me. Instead she looked straight ahead and said in her steady yet firm voice, "She's quite ok as she is, and she'll find her own way when she grows up".

Not another word was said on the subject and the teacher, that prophetess of gloom, dared not look my Mum in the eye.

In that instance, I worshipped my Mum. She was a Goddess in my eyes.

The fact that she didn't see the need to CHANGE me in any way, the fact that I was QUITE OK as I was, and that she trusted ME to FIND MY OWN WAY when I grew up, was music to my ears.

It may also give you some clues as to why I've always been an advocate for helping other women be true to themselves in all their weird and wonderful glory.

It may also explain why my first business was an image consulting business focused on helping women discover their own unique beauty and confidence to look and feel like the goddesses they are.

It may also explain why my second business is a coaching business, where I get to work with women from across the globe to help empower and call out their gifts and greatness from within.

I didn't fit the box. My mum didn't try to fit me into a box.

In fact years later, she would tell me that when I was 3.5 years old she KNEW that I would be independent, unconventional, and be someone who would do things their own way to make their own mark in the world.

So here I was poised for greatness. Ready to make my mark on the world.

And hearing this uplifting story, you might think that my future from that point onwards was glorious, and I was nurtured into greatness and the rest was history.

Not so fast.

Soon, things happened that broke my heart.

This took away some of my innocence and deeply ingrained some deadly stories that I told myself for years to come.

Feelings of unworthiness, unhappiness and that I was to blame for the pain I felt.

I've heard that if you've been through some sort of trauma, then hearing, seeing or reading about another person's traumatic experiences can make you feel as if you're going through the experience yourself.

This is especially true for the highly sensitive, compassionate and empathic souls amongst us (I'm one of those too), so in consideration of you, my beautiful soul, I will spare you the details here.

Suffice to say that from a young age, I felt so much pain.

I took on other people's pain on top of mine.

I mistrusted everyone including myself.

I started feeling a deep seated anger, slow burning but sudden and impetuous.

It would take me decades before I heard phrases like "Highly-Sensitive", "Empathic", and "Highly Intuitive", that described me to a tee, and helped me bring context and healing into why I felt the way I did.

Chapter 2

Spitfire

Soon any thoughts or memories of greatness took a backseat.

Instead came anger, determination, striving to prove myself and striving to prove anyone wrong should they dare challenge me on the basis of me being a skinny little brown immigrant girl.

See, my parents moved from a then war torn country of Sri Lanka, to the greener pastures of New Zealand when I was a kid.

All I knew about New Zealand in my young mind at the time was that they had loads of sheep, and made Anchor milk. So I imagined some sort of a place where you couldn't take a step without tripping on a sheep, abounding in rolling green hills, where I could drink lots of milk and own a farm.

Instead we grew up in the very average suburbs of West Auckland, and having not encountered racism before, I couldn't quite understand why I was asked by some kids at my new school whether we owned a dairy. (A corner store, for rest of the world)

A lot of the dairies in Auckland at the time was owned by Indian nationals, so those school kids were doubly wrong.

We didn't own a dairy and I wasn't an Indian!

I saw the sacrifices that my parents made and the indelible mark it left on them, so I was determined as hell to not be shaken by racial slurs or be pushed around by anyone.

I was always on the defense, on alert, always scanning my horizon for threats and taking care of them swiftly.

I was like one of those animals that puff themselves up so that they can look twice as big to scare away the predators.

Proving myself became the most important thing in the world for me.

That in itself is not a bad thing.

Except, mine was founded on a deep seated fear of not being good enough, not feeling loved, and hence feeling the need to protect myself from a world that was out to get me.

(Hark back to my teacher uttering those words "You'll never amount to anything", "You're not good enough")

I didn't feel like I was enough.

If it was just determination and drive, maybe I would have turned out to be a much better, or a well rounded person.

Except I had anger to deal with.

I'd feel rage bubbling up within me, feelings that I thought others may not even be capable of feeling.

The more I felt this way, the lower my opinion of myself became.

How can I be good, be responsible and make those I love proud of me, when I felt bad and broken on the inside?

When I felt rage, when I felt FEELINGS all the freaking time in a spectrum that other human beings seem oblivious to?

I felt too much, I cared too much and I would give my world to see other people happy and I was getting used by those who were far more street smart than I was.

So I deliberately fought those feelings, so I could feel less and care less.

As a child I had always been one of those sensitive souls who could feel energy, emotions, and troubles of others and saw it as my nature to be compassionate, to heal and empower others.

Instead I pushed all those feelings down. I will not be used. I will build an empire so my haters can cower and I would be self-sufficient and independent and then I would have proven myself.

Soon I had bottled up enough anger inside of me to the point I hadn't shed a tear in years and then things finally came to a head when I was at University.

Students are pretty broke to start off with, but even with my part time job, what money I made was leaving me faster than it came into my account.

I was trying to buy happiness for me and for those around me and failing miserably.

I had started going to a church at the time, feeling like my lost soul could be saved and nurtured back into health.

Among the church goers, I befriended this girl, who was an exemplary Christian by word, by deed, and by virtue.

She never had a bad word to say about anybody and was always so full of joy, and energy.

She was one of those people who looked like she had a permanent halo around her, angelic in nature and with a sweet soul to match.

It was to this vessel of greatness that I decided to talk about my money troubles.

I wasn't expecting anything from her, (I didn't expect anything from anyone, I didn't ask anyone for help. My motto was that there is no one to help me, and that I must help myself. Hello Miss Independent) I just wanted to share my heavy burden and the unhappiness I felt.

I think I was just short for rent that week.

Without any hesitation, she offered me $200 to make up the shortfall.

I remember choking up with emotion. It was a lot of money back then.

I remember refusing, but I remember most of all, her walking up to an ATM machine and withdrawing the money right there and then and she put it in my hand.

"Pay me when you can Rach. There's no hurry".

At that moment, I had a glimpse of greatness again.

The ability of a human being to shower happiness and hope on another human being by an expression of greatness.

And again we reach a point I could leave you feeling uplifted and tell you that my life changed at this point and the rest was history.

No, instead the story takes a turn...

A couple of weeks after, I had paid her back and we were walking and chatting together along one of the shaded lanes at the University. It was a gorgeous sunny day.

I can't even remember what we were talking about, but I remember, I suddenly became angry and blurted something out.

Actually it felt like an explosion of anger shooting out of me, spitting fire, burning anything it touched, corrosive in nature like acid.

The recipient of my wrath stopped in her tracks.

The next thing I recall is her face, sublime and serene like the moon, with a hint of sadness in her eyes as she looked at my angry face.

And then without a word, she walked away.

She wasn't angry, she knew her own power and saw my weakness for what it was.

She didn't holler at me, she chose not to engage in whatever anger-infused accusation I made, and she simply walked away.

As I stood there seeing her walk away, I remember my world crashing in slow motion around me.

My cheeks glowing, my heart racing, my head pounding and my world spinning.

It felt like I've spat on the face of a saint or committed some heinous crime, too vile to be forgiven.

How can I spit fire at someone who graciously lent me a helping hand when I needed it the most, only a few days ago?

How can I be this bad, this broken, and this awful inside?

How did I go from being poised for greatness to being the person who felt angry, hurt and out of control?

That was the day I acknowledged that something had to change.

I've been carrying around so much unhappiness, anger, and frustration that I've piled away for years and I had somehow turned into an angry person who shouts at a friend without any justifiable reason.

I knew that wasn't who I was deep down.

I remembered the glimpses that I've had into my own greatness as a child and I decided, that was my true nature.

Not being an angry, frustrated, unhappy, and hurt individual who hurts others, walking around like an open wound, and wincing at each turn because all I could feel was my pain.

I've heard people talk about having "anger management issues", so I decided perhaps that's what I had.

I don't know, maybe I had nothing of the kind, just a whole lot of pain, confusion and frustration doing its damage at a soul level, that needed to be cleared out.

I decided to take action and start dealing with what was beneath the surface.

I finally shed tears I've been holding back for years.

I apologised, I started journaling my thoughts, I started breathing deeply and releasing emotion.

I started singing more and writing more, poetry, songwriting, prose, anything that came to mind that helped me give expression to myself again.

I started healing myself by giving myself permission to be ME.

Therein lies the not so secret, secret to unleashing your greatness.

PART 2

Chapter 3

Unleashing Greatness

At this point I want to check in with you because this part is all about you.

It is also about asking an important question.

How in the world do you unleash your greatness?

I mean, doesn't that sound a little bit cheesy even?

Having lost my sense of greatness every now and then and having powerfully unleashed it in my life at other times, as a performer, writer, speaker and a coach, I know that the story of greatness is one that needs to be written with deliberation.

And that means willingness to lay aside everything that you thought was your reality and dig so deep within until you find an entire well of crystal clear and pure greatness that you've hidden underneath layers of fear, threats, abuse, addictions and pain.

You may have even covered it up with a layer of mundane womanly duties that you thought you are supposed to be doing.

On top of that is a layer of how you should be, how you should act, look, and think as a person as dictated by everything you see around you.

So you see peeling layers takes courage, and just like when you peel onions, you might get the tears flowing and the emotional release that you've been too afraid to allow yourself to feel so far.

So...if you're willing for it to get messy, challenging, and soul searching, this is a good place to start.

Greatness is already within you.

Whether you like it or not. Whether you believe it or not. Whether you acknowledge it or not.

The same way, dark matter exists in space which we cannot see (making up a whopping 85% of the total mass of our universe) and even though billions of dollars of research and centuries of observation by some of the greatest scientific minds still haven't been able to understand or define it well.

Scientists only know of its gigantic, powerful and yet invisible properties, by the way it exerts its influence on the physical universe.

Greatness also is not a physical and a tangible thing that we can put in a box and say "that's greatness".

We know of its existence by the influence it exerts on us, powerful, relentless at times, and the undeniable effect it has on us and anyone who comes into contact with us, if we allow it to flow freely through us.

Greatness can't be manufactured. If it's attempted, you only create a superficial, and a hollow frame that is as fragile as glass and it will not survive the test of time.

Have you ever felt greatness?

Whether you feel like you have or not, we won't make much progress into unleashing greatness unless you believe that...

Greatness is already within you.

The first step is to first and foremost believe that.

We catch glimpses of it when we yearn to be a better version of ourselves.

Not in a perfectionistic, keeping up with the joneses kind of way.

But in a deep, powerful, inspiring yearning that calls us to action, and calls us to start bringing our most impossible dreams into reality.

The yearning we feel in our heart that tells us that we are born for more, meant for more and capable of more than what we are right now.

You see it when you get 'crazy' ideas about changing the world, building a school for orphans, ending child slavery, building an empowered coalition of women who were victims of abuse, becoming a world renowned healer...

Those thoughts that you get, that you feel incredible about for a moment, thrilled at the prospect of being a vessel through which greatness, change and healing can flow and then you promptly listen to your doubts or Who-do-you-think-you-are moments push away the calling of greatness and settle back into 'reality'.

Greatness can flow within you in the stillness of your heart, it can consume you, or it can simply wrap you in its arms and whisper what you've always known to be true.

That you are born for greatness.

All of this happens by a simple, profound and a confounding truth.

You must ALLOW Greatness.

What do I mean by this?

What it exactly sounds like.

You mean if I don't ALLOW greatness, and block it somehow and keep it buried under a lot of layers, it won't do its thing?

That's exactly what I mean.

There's no magic or sorcery to that. Just pure common sense.

If you push down your greatness, it won't somehow push back against you, give you a swift uppercut, tackle you to the ground and unleash itself onto the world through you.

I wish it did, but that will take away YOUR power of choice as a human being.

Our ability to choose for ourselves is a big part of what makes us human, so no, we can't take that away from you.

I mentioned earlier that somehow as we grow up, being in our natural element, feeling and unleashing our greatness in a way that's most natural to us, tends to put the society's nose out of joint.

It becomes a faux pas to acknowledge one's own greatness.

It becomes cool and loveable to become self-deprecating, always championing others and diminishing oneself, and making sacrifices for others.

I remember an example of this, when someone told me about one of his mates and his girlfriend.

Friend: (with admiration), "you know, so and so (mate's girlfriend)?"

Me: "yeah"

Friend: "Well my mate can be a pain in the ass sometimes, he plays up, loses his temper, and is so difficult, but she puts up with all of that and doesn't say a word and cooks for him when he turns up. She's really nice and is perfect for him".

Me: (in disbelief and possibly glaring at him) "So…she puts up with crap from him all the time, and doesn't say a word and always ready with a cooked meal for him, and that makes her really nice? What about him? Why can't he be nice too for a change? She needs to stand up for herself."

Friend: (Blank stare)

What I want to show you is that as we get older we transition from being the centre of attention, entertaining our family with our childhood performances and not feeling ashamed for being complemented for confidence and self-love to needing to please everybody around us, sacrifice ourselves for other people's happiness and give up our innate desire to do and be an expression of greatness.

Don't get me wrong, there is nothing wrong with service, humility and compassion for others. In fact my life's purpose is very much tied around to being of service to others. So I'm not talking about that.

I'm talking about the fact that if you diminish yourself long enough for the sake of others, you lose yourself. Fully and completely. Until you won't know yourself.

And where your true nature disappears to, greatness also will follow suit.

And it will remain hidden until you damn well insist that you'll unleash your greatness and won't rest until you elevate your own true nature, that gives you joy, and keeps you happy and fulfilled and helps you choose a path that gives you the ultimate self-expression.

So instead of pushing it down, turning it away when it softly nudges you and reminds you of its existence, start paying attention like never before.

Drop everything and pay attention.

If you get good at ignoring your greatness long enough, the longer the timing between the soft nudges will become until it is barely detectable.

If you become good at ignoring it when your heart leaps for joy when you're thinking of building that school for street kids in Mexico, the lesser it will come into your heart or your mind after a while.

If you get good at ignoring the signs that push you towards greater happiness in your relationship through more honesty, and you keep yourself from rocking the boat, the less you will feel the tug at your heart, until one day you suddenly wonder why you spent a lifetime in a relationship, where its full potential was never realized and you've had the breakup from hell to show for it.

So let me spell it out here.

What you feel inside of you is REAL.

You can run away from it for as long as you like, but greatness will always try to remind you of its existence within you.

You might get very good at shutting it up when it shows, and the distance between the calls may become longer, but it will try to remind you, what you came here to do, until your dying day.

But it will respect and rely on YOUR CHOICE as to when it can be unleashed.

You can find a thousand reasons as to why you can't tap into and unleash your greatness.

There is no time.

I'm too tired after work.

The bills need to be paid.

This is a big risk.

People will laugh at me.

What if I fall flat on my face and go bankrupt?

What if...what if...what if...

Let me break it down for you here.

Do you think that those people that you admire, those other people who are out there being successful and owning their greatness, did it once all the clouds cleared and the Red sea parted for them?

Do you think they waited until they had a few thousand dollars lying around to start a business?

Did they wait for sunny skies and perfect room temperature before asking the one they love if they would marry them?

Do you think they waited until their lives were perfect and blissful before they took massive leaps of faith and that they landed on a big soft cushion and experienced no pain?

I'm being facetious and for good reason.

Unleashing greatness requires working towards emotional maturity.

That means when you feel like throwing a tantrum, even with good reason, you reflect, you redirect your energy towards being the best version of yourself.

That means when you feel justified in feeling sorry for yourself, you choose to step away from self-pity and move towards a higher ground of self-empowerment.

Many of us admire those who have gone before us and have unleashed their greatness and inspire us to do the same, but we can make the stupidest excuses as to why it can't happen to us, why not now, why not here, why we are not worthy, why it wouldn't work and God knows what else.

If only my darling, you realised that unleashing greatness doesn't require perfection.

In fact it's often moments of great change, great honesty, great crises, and great decision that provides the prime conditions for greatness to come to surface and unleash as it senses your newfound enthusiasm for life, despite your circumstances.

This is also the great secret of manifesting whatever you desire in your heart.

It's that feeling when you hit rock bottom and you know you can't go further and the only way is now up.

It's being grateful for the life you have when that is all you have left.

It's about dreaming and obsessing over having a first class culinary feast at a Five Star Restaurant be your normal when in reality you're down to your last $20 eating bread and butter in your tiny little apartment. (I did and it was the moment where I left a job I hated, doubled my income within a few weeks and gave me the courage to start my first business and get 120 clients in one week)

It's about being kind and compassionate before you feel like a Saint and before you have all your sins washed away and before you feel new.

It's about writing as if you're the next bestselling author even if you don't have two pennies to rub together.

Speak to your walls as if you're the next Martin Luther King Jr. addressing and inspiring a nation, when you're living in a tiny little studio apartment and you don't know where your next rent payment is coming from. (I did)

Listen to the constant nudges you've received in your heart and mind about what sets your soul on fire.

Reflect and look back to what your heart has always desired, unfailingly, and undiminished during all those years.

Your greatness looks different to my greatness and yet it's the same feelings, desires, yearnings, that will try to get your attention, to bring you back to your core and to your authentic self.

Where your greatness lies.

Chapter 4

Your Heart's Desires

Have you ever noticed how easy it is to put yourself down, pick holes in your creative work, blame yourself for the unhappiness of others, and notice how you've put on an extra few kg's in the last couple of weeks, and feel terrible that you're not spending enough time with your loved ones?

This list can go on...we can find 1000 different ways to make ourselves feel bad, feel guilty, blame ourselves, and punish ourselves.

When we do that, we labour under a false premise.

That it's normal to feel that way.

In fact, when you feel like that, you're essentially as far away from being in touch with your true nature as possible.

Your feelings are your ultimate guide to showing you how far you've wandered off the path that feels right, that feels good to the core of your soul, and the path of being and embodying the qualities of the person that you wish to be.

If it doesn't feel good, then it's not aligned to who you are at your core.

Doesn't that make everything simpler?

Imagine, that instead of noticing everything that you think is wrong with you, that all of a sudden you start to notice that you are all but human like the rest of us.

That you look at yourself with eyes of compassion and love for the first time, acknowledging that the pain, the joy and all the life experiences you've had that has brought you here.

Not because you're flawed.

Not because you're broken.

Not because you're unloved.

Not because you're not good enough.

Now imagine this...and if you've never experienced a time like this, I want you to imagine what it would be like.

Take yourself back to a time where you felt your heart soaring inside of you, excited by possibilities and fully believed that you were born for a purpose and that there was goodness, purpose and a fire that burned so bright within you that could change the world.

Imagine that instead of noticing what you haven't done well or right, instead you started to notice that it was possible to feel that good again.

That it's possible that you are inherently good and made for greatness.

And that you started to ALLOW that greatness to come through, to show up...by doing what sets your heart on fire.

In its purest, unadulterated, and fiercest form, you come to realise that you are BORN for greatness?

Do you see what I did there?

I literally talked myself away from feeling bad, from wallowing in my current situation or my very real pain, towards questions that took me closer to what my true nature and core would want me to feel.

Those questions took me back to believing there is greatness within me, and that no matter what the circumstances that I can start being true to myself and start being happy, authentic and aligned starting right now.

Instead of waiting for someone to come and make your pain go away.

Even if someone could do that for a short period, you can never push down what you haven't faced up to.

It will always show up and in a way be a reminder to try and lead you back to where you truly belong.

Most of us live our entire lives, wanting to get to that certain place where we are a better version of ourselves, perhaps our spouse and kids are a better version of themselves, and the world as a whole is a better version of itself.

A place where we are always happy, a place where we are skinny and healthy, a place where we eat chocolate for breakfast, lunch and dinner and don't put on any weight, and a place where we act in accordance with our principles at all times.

A place where you are being the best version of yourself.

A place where you have the freedom to do whatever it is that you want.

A place where your dreams become reality with ease.

This mythical place is always in our hearts and in our minds, tantalisingly close at times and for most of us feels hopelessly far away most of the time.

That's why when we evaluate our current situation of being angry, frustrated, hopeless, unhappy, hurt, disillusioned, or anything else, that you feel as far away from the mythical place that you are trying to somehow "get" to.

Instead imagine that you started BEING who you think you will be if you had everything you ever asked for.

Imagine yourself being the best selling author.

Imagine yourself being the inspiring speaker, who's receiving a thundering applause from a crowd you just set alight with inspiration.

Imagine yourself being that person embodying everything you secretly wish you were...

What we feel in our hearts, the truth that we don't acknowledge even to our spouses is that we feel a tug at our very hearts that excites us about being this person.

Now let's make it clear again, there is a difference between greatness and perfection.

The innermost desires we feel in our hearts, felt in our heart since we were children, point to the imprint of greatness within.

A greatness that is wholesome, empowering, and inspiring.

A greatness that is creative, playful and isn't aware of rules and restrictions.

A greatness that isn't structured, planned out or controlled according to what you or anyone else says.

See...that's why you're only chasing a superficial and a shadow version of greatness when you desire perfection.

True greatness demolishes any notions of perfection.

Because it requires you to start from where you are and unleash from today.

Not after you've got your s#%^ sorted.

Not after you write better songs.

Not after you write better books.

Not after your relationship is sorted.

Not after you got your business idea locked down.

Not after you feel whole inside.

Right now.

I KNOW that the inclinations I had as a child about inner greatness, my ability to inspire and change people's lives through my words were ALL the information I ever needed to fulfill my purpose, succeed and win in life, and be happy to my very core.

And yet, the world kinda got in the way, and made me think that I needed to do something else, be someone else, and live another life.

Isn't it mad?

I've found peace by coming to terms with what life has been so far, and I've found inspiration by finding out that no matter how unpromising a start you or others think you made in life.

Where you are right now is the best place to start unleashing greatness, to start being true and to acknowledge that what you feel in your heart is REAL and it will no longer be denied.

It's about you as you are right now.

Do it today. There is nothing stopping you.

Nothing unleashes greatness more than the knowledge that you are no slave to circumstance.

So whatever your circumstances are, get clear and pay attention to what your heart's desires has been, especially as a child, before the world left its mark on you.

Therein lies your greatness.

Paraphrasing the great Gary Vaynerchuck, you need to look in the mirror, and ask yourself what's the purest form of YOU is, and build your life based on the answer to that and give it full expression.

Chapter 5

What It Takes

This in its turn, if you allow it, starts defining you.

And the way you live each day and starts transforming you from the inside out.

Because you tried a couple of times and greatness didn't unleash according to your expectations, is no reason to give up and throw in the towel.

So I need to tell you about what it takes to unleash greatness.

Daily.

Consistently.

In a massive way.

A woman of greatness, does not run and hide when the going gets tough. Even if she feels like running and hiding or crying into a box of Eucalyptus scented tissues. (that's me I'm talking about)

A woman of greatness allows her greatness to flow even in difficult times, so that she is reminded of who she truly is and what immense, untold, and impossible adventures she is capable of bringing to life.

A woman of greatness, always refers back to the fact that she was born for greatness and no hell fire or snowstorm changes the fact that greatness is within her, available to be called upon, at a moment's notice.

Even if right now you feel like royalty in rags, roaming the wilderness like King Nebuchadnezzar, allowing the expression of greatness means that you don't forget yourself and who you were born to be.

And that's why nothing excites me more than helping women unleash their greatness through the incredible gifts, stories, creativity and passions that they bring to the world.

Do you wonder how some people build a fierce and loyal following whether in large or small communities?

It happens because they allow their greatness to shine through their personality, in their words and in their actions.

Other people see something in them that they would like to express, allow and live out for themselves.

They allow greatness by being bold with their message, and they don't edit who they are and share both strength and vulnerability while staying true to their heart's desires.

Daily. Consistently. In a massive way.

We are drawn to women and men who do this, we idolize them, we look up to them and that's how they get their audience of raving mad fans.

That's what others call luck, natural leadership or charisma.

The fact is they've tapped into their greatness and that they allow greatness to be expressed through them without limits or reservation.

This is why there is no point in trying to replicate other people, other brands or what other people are doing.

You have your own brand of greatness that you need to call forth from deep within yourself.

Full expression of greatness requires daily decisions in favour of YOUR brand of greatness.

Even when you have the option to say, no I don't feel like owning my greatness today or acting in accordance with my greatness.

When you feel like hitting snooze on your alarm clock, when you feel like reaching for another chocolate croissant, when you feel like not putting yourself out there to be visible and shining your light in a way that people can't miss you a mile away.

Expression of greatness looks different for everyone, but we know it when we see it.

We are magnetically drawn to it, perhaps to people who are very different from who you are, simply because you feel the greatness that they carry and allow themselves to live in.

My Coach is just such a person, a fierce leader with a no-bullshit attitude, a whirlwind of energy and power.

She doesn't shy away from telling it like it is, kicking people's asses, giving value or selling to her audience.

She knows that she provides bucket loads of value and she's a phenomenal leader with crazy loyal followers who buy every little thing or every big thing that she ever produces.

It's like she can't lose.

Now as much as I'd want to emulate her and do stuff that she does, my brand of greatness looks vastly different to hers so it's up to me to dig deep and find my own brand of greatness as it were.

Mine is a passion that burns bright within and people get to see it when I'm in flow and in alignment and doing what I love.

I'm an introvert to my core, but my flamboyance, my love of performance, arts, and writing gives away the colourful inner world that I only allow a very few people into.

I've always known that I have a calming and a healing effect on people and that's why people in distress seek me out.

My light shines brightest when I can encourage others and when I can build up others to see and express their own greatness.

I have lots of ideas in my head on a daily basis, which are all running at 100 miles an hour and it gives me immense pleasure to be doing about 10 projects in parallel.

Your brand of greatness might be vastly different to both of the snippets of examples I've given.

Your mission, should you choose to accept it, is to get in touch with your greatness and to allow it to flow until it becomes as natural as your breathing.

I know people who spend years trying to hone in on what their passions are, what their purpose in life is, and why they are here on this planet.

I was that person.

The longer I ignored what I had always known, the longer the answer to those big questions seem to elude me.

Not being able to hone in on one passion, one niche, one purpose, one package, one neat little thing that I was known for, was one of the most excruciating experiences that I put myself through.

Why?

Everybody else said that's how you do it so I was trying to conform to other people's rules.

That's how you build a business.

That's how you attract your audience.

That's how you do what you love to do and make a living out of it.

That's what entrepreneurs are supposed to do.

That's what you need to do to be successful.

That's what you do in life to get ahead.

Except...

It's all a load of utter bollocks.

It just took me YEARS to figure out. Even though I've always known it on the inside.

I had become very good at suppressing my own truth and allowing other people's voices and opinions to be greater than my inner voice and inner truth.

The pressure is immense at times to look at what others are doing and be infuriated about why I don't fit into a nice, neat little box like others do.

When others made quick sales, bragged about their $10 gazillion dollar month, or talked about the best freaking Holy Grail strategy in the world, it was infuriating to just sit there and speak my truth day in and day out.

To allow myself to be a creative and a healing soul first and foremost.

To trust that the brand of greatness I bring to this world is one that other people are crying out for, if only I wouldn't buckle under the pressure to look, speak, sound, write and be like other people and how THEY are doing it.

To know in your heart that what you've always known to be your truth, doesn't change just because someone else got

10,000 instagram followers in one week and hit the big time and you didn't.

If you've read this far, and if you resonated with what I said about being the unconventional, diamond in the rough, one of a kind, do things your way kinda person, then...

You know you are born for greatness.

You know you have a message that could empower the masses.

You know you are born to be a leader.

You know that nothing fulfills you more than being connected to your soul and expressing yourself and your art and your message and releasing it into the world.

You know that you don't fit into a box.

You know that your emotions run wild ranging from fierce loyalty, to burning rage to herculean strength and exemplary courage that others rely on.

You know you're different.

You see things that others don't see, patterns, behaviours and connections and an uncanny intuitive ability that reveals the innermost thoughts and feelings of other people.

You know that you are born for greatness.

And yet, at this very moment, you could be in the throes of self-doubt, a familiar companion that's been by your side as far as you can remember.

The soul of an artist is a complex one, and in our eagerness to express our art, our message, and not being able to do it in a conventional, entrepreneurial, money making way, immediately, is enough to make you want to throw in the towel, howl in despair, shake your fists towards heaven and simply walk away from it all.

The only problem is, you know that you're not likely to have any peace for the rest of your life if you decide to ignore your calling.

Your greatness CANNOT be denied.

Your greatness WILL NOT be denied.

If you've been called to greatness, no matter how hard you push it down and even if you manage to quiet the constant tug at your heart, it inevitably comes back.

And it hurts more to not listen, it drives you crazy to ignore it, and it turns you madder than a hatter who is desperately looking for answers to this maddening puzzle.

You feel like you haven't figured something out.

That you've missed a piece of the information that other people are somehow privy to.

So you end up hoarding more knowledge, more information, more courses, more coaches, and more strategies into your life, until you drown out your own inner voice.

The problem is, that while the calling of your heart remains persistent, greatness simply can't express itself when you allow yourself to be buried beneath layers and layers of conventional wisdom.

It doesn't come into expression when you finally "grow up" and decide it's your lot in life to blend into a boring shade of grey.

When you take pieces of this strategy, that coach, that book and try and piece it together to make it work for you.

It doesn't.

It won't.

It will look nothing like YOU.

For greatness to thrive, it requires an environment of acceptance.

Acceptance that you are born for greatness.

That means that you Think, Do, and Act like someone who is born for greatness.

Not tomorrow when you're ready. Today, damn it, TODAY.

Do the work that it takes to clear up years of training that we've inflicted on ourselves to fit into some form of a civilized human being.

No I'm not asking you to be uncivilized.

I'm asking you to release the wildness that you've learned to tame.

I'm asking you to be ok with doing things differently to how OTHER PEOPLE do it.

I'm asking you to unleash your greatness like this is the last chance you'll ever get.

Greatness takes courage.

If it was easy, everyone would be doing it right?

The fact is it's not easy to cut through years of bull shit that you've been telling yourself.

It's downright difficult to accept that you don't fit into one neat little package, when you're a multi passionate, multi talented, one woman freakshow that nobody has ever seen!

That's ok though.

That sounds like the exact conditions for greatness to thrive, and find expression and finally unleash itself on an unsuspecting world.

So this is where we turn the corner.

We take a step, or rather you take a step to finally decide to no longer live a pretend, make believe or an easy version of the real life you are supposed to live.

To live with courage, to be bold with your message even if you're an introvert or if you quake in your boots every time you step up to a stage or get in front of people.

Even if the thought of doing what you love, and taking risks, being more honest than you have ever been with yourself makes you come all over with hives.

It's time to UNLEASH your greatness.

Chapter 6

The Power of Your Thoughts

Greatness takes courage, greatness takes work, and greatness is for those who act.

BUT...

Greatness is not meant to be hard to unleash.

It's not meant to be something that takes years of practise, and lots of qualifications and letters after your name.

So why do we find it difficult to flow right into what we are born to do and live a life of absolute expression of your greatness?

The difficulty doesn't lie with Greatness itself.

It's the years of training that you need to unlearn, and allowing yourself to be FULLY you, that's downright HARD.

Isn't that just mad?

That's because it takes some discovery and some exploration into the unchartered territories within yourself.

It takes a David Attenborough level of curiosity and an Anthony Robbins level of energy to venture into the unknown.

The good news is that you don't have to have all of that figured out upfront.

You just have to start right now, from precisely the place where you are at right now.

One of the greatest methods of unleashing greatness that I know of is journaling or writing, and there are many other methods too.

So whatever your thoughts are on journaling, and whatever prejudices that come to mind, I'd like you to lay them aside for a minute and invite you to give it a go right now.

The level of inner work required to cut through layers of defenses, behaviours, habits and attitudes that you have entertained for so long, takes work but journaling is a powerful tool that clears away that overgrown thicket of your mind to get to where the vein of gold lies.

So, let's start by asking a question…

What's your definition of yourself?

There are thousands of thoughts that you think on a daily basis, where if it becomes habitual, you don't even notice what the thoughts say anymore.

That's because your habitual reinforcement of the thoughts has turned it into a deeply ingrained BELIEF.

You're useless.

Who am I to think I can build a life where I'm deliriously happy and fulfilled?

Why haven't you figured it out? Other people have.

Stop being soft. This will take hard work and grunt to make it happen and a lot of struggle. Just harden the F#%^ up.

Greatness indeed. Why don't you have some more chocolate cake?

I could go on, but I won't.

You may have your own very long list of thoughts that you think of on a daily basis.

The only way to sort out the thoughts and to see them for the soul-destroying, utterly useless and mocking changelings they are is to get them out of your head and onto paper.

At first, you may be like how I was first, picking up a pen and paper and not having any idea what to say, and feeling stupid because of that.

But you have to start, you have to get that pen and start writing words on that paper before magic can start to happen.

My journaling pages at the start looked like this:

"I don't know what to write so I'll just keep writing I guess, and I'm super sleepy and tired but apart from that I don't know what else to write, am I ever gonna find anything useful to write. I don't know what to write, so I'll just keep writing, I don't know what to write so I'll just keep writing..."

I would write that for pages upon pages before my resisting mind would finally give up and open up the floodgates of thoughts onto the page.

I would write anything and everything. Without judgment, without editing, without crossing out a single word.

Even if you sound like a whining, pathetic, master of complaints, keep writing.

Even if your life as it is now sounds bleak and looks like there is no hope, keep writing.

Even when your heart fails, because you can't see the light after all these long years, keep writing.

You're simply clearing out the forest at this stage to prepare the field to grow and birth the greatest harvest of greatness you've ever seen yet.

Allow your mind to empty itself onto the page. (I used to write 3 x A4 pages each morning, my current journal is A5 so I write more pages now.)

Slowly I could start seeing glimpses of clarity.

My incoherent mind babble turned into coherent words on the page, and I'd ask myself questions, ordering my brain to find the answer during the writing time or during the day.

What am I so afraid of?

Why do I find it so hard to forgive?

Why am I the way I am?

It's like the forest was cleared away and I was digging away at the hard ground to prepare it for the seeds of greatness I was about to sow.

I would then start receiving the answers to my own questions. Answers that I hadn't been brave enough to look in the face before.

Brutal at times, but mostly inexpressible relief at being able to tackle the deepest, darkest scars and wounds that have lay hidden beneath the surface.

To bring them to the light, and start washing away the wounds, treating them with healing balms, wrapping them up with the gentlest love and finally begin the process of rejuvenation and rebirth.

As I persisted with writing each morning, before I got up (yes I was writing while lying in bed), it's like the ground hardened with years of soul famine, slowly started to become soft and supple again, and now I could freely plant the seeds.

My writing shifted from complaints and frequent allusions to how tired I am, to feeling excited and acknowledging the reawakening I was starting to feel within.

Slowly but surely I would write, like one possessed, often not noticing how long it took before having to rush off to work.

Soon I was reaping a harvest that yielded the fruits of my labour and it was the greatest I had seen at that time.

It felt as if I've found my way back home. And it only got better from there.

I've recognised my authentic self, like a long lost friend.

Like a wild haired lover that I was torn from a long time ago, reunited in ecstatic tears and joy.

I started to be and embody the person that I knew I was born to be.

A Woman of Greatness.

Not a woman of sorrow.

Not a woman of pain.

Not a woman of low self-esteem.

A Woman of Greatness.

Let me clear something up here.

Don't get me wrong, I don't just think thoughts of greatness ALL the time and never trip up or never make mistakes.

Even as I wrote the above line "A Woman of Greatness", a thought flashed across my mind.

Arrogant.

And it may well seem arrogant to other people as well.

Years of conditioning, psychologically, socially through nature or nurture, you've come to believe that it's not acceptable to reach for the glorious feeling of wholeness that you crave, and find it inside of you because that would set you above others and make you look arrogant.

Isn't it normal for people to be broken, to be hurt, and to feel pain?

So how dare I think that my life could somehow be different to that?

How dare I demand that my life be full of purpose, inspiration, creativity, laughter and happiness?

At the end of the day, it's up to YOU to decide how much you care about being seen to be part of the pack and how much you'd value that above your purpose, your happiness and your greatness.

To blend into a shade of gray that no one recognises, while you wither inside while still longing to burst into a thousand colour rainbow.

None of us want to admit it but the reason we don't step up and dazzle the world with our greatness is because we are simply afraid of what other people might say or think of us.

I mean, wouldn't they think that I'm some arrogant, self-centered BIATCH!

Wouldn't my family be ashamed at my big ego after all their efforts to raise me up to be a polite and a nice person?

What would my clients or my tribe think? They probably think "Who does she think she is to be all high and mighty"?

While we run these what-if, worst-case, end-of-the-world type scenarios in our heads, greatness takes a back seat and is paralysed as it cannot move without our permission.

Chapter 7

Permission

That last word. PERMISSION.

It really comes down to whether we allow ourselves each day to take the path of greatness or take the path of least resistance into familiarity and comfort where you don't ruffle any feathers, where you think about everyone else's comfort, while YOU my darling, wither away on the inside.

You are like a caged bird, with a tropical plume that you can't spread or show because you're confined by the terms and conditions that you put on yourself or allow others to put upon you.

A glorious creature like you was never meant to be in a cage, self-devised or otherwise.

A place where no one can see your beauty, your courage, and your glorious self.

A place where you are forced to quiet your voice, your message and your calling to empower the masses.

See...I hope you are starting to realise that there is no magical 7 step formula to unleash your greatness.

But ALLOWING yourself PERMISSION to EMBODY and EXPRESS greatness has everything to do with whether you live out your purpose or whether you choose to dull your shine in fear of bedazzling those around you.

It's necessary to think of greatness in these lofty terms.

Most people go about their lives without ever thinking about the fact that they are created for greatness.

Mortgages, kids, career, partying, and plain mundane busyness takes over and any spare time left over is taken up by that great inducer of dullness: television.

There is a reason why we feel like failures on the inside, there is a reason, why we eat, drink, watch TV, do drugs, allow drama into our lives or do whatever it takes to numb the pain that this truth brings.

That we are not living the life we know we are capable of living.

That we are not living in alignment to our core values.

That we are not allowing our greatness the freedom of expression it deserves and it craves to express in our lives.

Personally I don't want to find out that I've lived a life of mediocrity when I could have lived with a glorious sense of purpose, happiness and alignment to my very core.

I don't want to wake up years later and find out that my life has been spent in doing what I thought I SHOULD be doing, instead of allowing my greatness to unleash each day to do what I was BORN to do.

I can't even imagine the pain I would feel to know that when I could have made a decision to allow greatness years ago, that I chose to remain quiet, to remain nice, to remain balanced and stable when in reality I'm an untamed wild beast on the inside fighting a raging battle each day to find expression.

Don't set yourself up for a lifetime of regrets.

Greatness awaits.

It's time to do something that you would think as too audacious, too arrogant or too flashy to do.

For me the words, wild, untamed, expressive, are words that make my heart sing.

So I want you to think up words that light up your heart when you hear them.

Write as many words as delights you! I have quite a few, so here's a list to get you started.

Empowering. Inspiring. Whirlwind. Force. Brilliance. Flamboyant. Glamourous. Cheeky. Fun. Elegant. Beautiful. Queen. Warrior. Fairy.

As you're writing, pay attention to any resistance you feel to CLAIMING a word as your own.

Thoughts of worthiness, self-doubt, false humility, lack of confidence, and more will surface but I want you to notice what comes up and then simply move on to write down your words anyway.

Isn't it funny that we can allow ourselves hours of lecturing, abuse and self-flagellation but the moment we write 3 empowering words about ourselves, all hell breaks loose?

That's RESISTANCE.

Resistance to being great.

Resistance to making a claim.

Resistance to drawing a line in the sand.

Resistance to commit.

Resistance to be powerful.

Resistance to be authentic.

Resistance to be the woman you know you are capable of being, if you weren't so afraid.

My job is to not sugar coat it or say things in a nice way or even write in a way that's conventional.

My purpose is to hold a mirror up to you so you can see your own greatness reflected back, the same greatness you've been hiding away in a closet all these years.

How does it look?

Is it scary?

Is it exciting?

Is it exhilarating?

Is it freeing?

Is it refreshing?

Is it anything you expected it would be?

Coming face to face with your own greatness is life-changing.

Even as I write, my heart is beating faster each minute because I know what it's like to be faced with my own greatness.

To feel as if I don't deserve it, to feel as if I should run away, to feel as if I could never do it justice.

Greatness, like inspiration and creativity only thrives in places where it has permission to thrive.

Where it has permission to express freely and fully.

This means you let go of trying to know all the answers beforehand.

This means letting go of preconceived ideas of what success looks like.

This means letting go of your inner need to have everything fenced in and under your control.

This is excruciating for a control freak like me.

But each day, when I allow greatness to take over, I feel things that I have never felt.

I feel a confidence that consumes me, and an inspiration that can't be explained.

Others are drawn to it, they want to know more about it, and they want whatever it is that I have.

It has nothing to do with being perfect and having everything figured out.

It has everything to do with the greatness I allow myself to express and being endowed with the gift of awakening greatness in others, not hiding in the shadows and giving of my gift and service, just as I am, exactly from where I am.

To take the mantle of a warrior, a fighter, a Queen, a wild thing, that cares fiercely about humanity, empowerment of women and expression of self.

So what is the mantle of greatness that you will take upon yourself today?

What warrior, Goddess, freak show, are you going to allow yourself to become if you're going to heed the call within, and to truly be YOU?

To do what makes your heart sing.

To hustle past the obstacles when they get in your way.

To push past fear and self-doubt day in and day out.

To shine so bright that you become a GLORIOUOS lighthouse in whatever corner of the world you're in.

Embodying and allowing your greatness doesn't mean you become fearless. It means you act despite fear. With your knees trembling, with your heart sinking in your stomach, with your skin turning cold.

Expressing greatness doesn't mean you have to wear the latest fashion and become a full fledged demanding diva to get your message across. It means you wear your $20 dress with confidence knowing that you're true to yourself and that you shine like a diamond.

Expressing greatness means that each day you get up with certainty that come hell or high water, you will not deviate from the course and the dreams that you have set for yourself.

Expressing greatness means that when you feel the pressure to conform, to perform, to be like everybody else, you still show up and stick out like a sore thumb in all your glorious weirdness.

Expressing greatness means that when you feel like turning it down a notch so that other people don't feel bad, or you don't make them look bad, you reveal a full beam of bedazzling light and refuse to be dragged down into the dark.

Expressing greatness means answering the call that you feel deep down, that you were made for greatness, that you were born to create and give expression to your full glory, without apology.

Expressing greatness means that you give yourself permission to be unashamedly YOU, follow your heart and its call when everybody else is following a 7 step formula to success, health or happiness.

You may have realised by now that what works for other people, doesn't quite work for you.

Sure it might bring in a few sales, it might get you a half decent relationship, it might make you generally happy.

But it doesn't make you want to explode into the night sky and outshine all the stars and to live out your life in a way that sends out a clear signal.

I accept my own greatness.

I give myself permission to unleash greatness in my life.

I allow greatness to flow through me each and every day.

I allow myself to live the life of impact I have always dreamed of, being a changemaker, a conduit of greatness and empower others with my message.

Greatness awaits.

So how about it?

Where are you at right now in terms of accepting and allowing greatness to flow in your own life?

Are you now convinced that you're not crazy and that what you've always felt deep down is the true calling of your heart and greatness looking for ways to find expression in your life?

I can't wait for you to shine your brilliance for all to see.

I can't wait to see you, finally not only be ok with who you are but celebrate each day that you have listened to the calling of your heart and that you recognise greatness within yourself and others.

You're no caged bird and there's nothing that can hold you back from taking flight and spreading your beautiful array of colours, personality, message, weirdness, power, impact, and love to a world that desperately needs it.

Greatness awaits.

If you start down this path, you might as well know that there's no turning back.

After all, once you've tasted the freedom that comes with allowing yourself full expression, forgiving all your past mistakes, and moving on to glorious expression of greatness, you would NEVER want to go back.

You've found where you belong, where your heart sings and where your greatness has full expression.

I have to take Marianne Williamson's words to be able to fully express what this means and leave you with this:

"Our deepest fear is not that we are inadequate.

Our deepest fear is that we are powerful beyond measure.

It is our light, not our darkness that most frightens us.

We ask ourselves, 'Who am I to be brilliant, gorgeous, talented, fabulous?'

Actually, who are you not to be?

You are a child of God.

Your playing small does not serve the world.

There is nothing enlightened about shrinking so that other people won't feel insecure around you.

We are all meant to shine, as children do.

We were born to make manifest the glory of God that is within us.

It's not just in some of us; it's in everyone.

And as we let our own light shine, we unconsciously give other people permission to do the same.

As we are liberated from our own fear, our presence automatically liberates others."

Greatness awaits.